My name is Maria. I am a girl.
Je m'appelle Maria. Je suis une jeune fille.

I am Spanish and I live in Spain.
Je suis espagnole et j'habite en Espagne

I have dark hair and green eyes.
J'ai les cheveux noirs et les yeux verts.

I have one brother. He is a pianist. My mother is a singer.
J'ai un frère. Il est pianiste. Maman est chanteuse.

I like playing tennis, riding my bicycle, and reading books.
J'aime le tennis, le vélo and la lecture.

bell
la sonnette

brake
le frein

handlebars
le guidon

tire
le pneu

THE BERENSTAIN BEARS

B297

THIS BOOK BELONGS TO

BECKY SEGAL

WORDBOOK
IN ENGLISH & FRENCH

GALLERY BOOKS
An Imprint of W. H. Smith Publishers Inc.
112 Madison Avenue
New York City 10016

Different
Throughout [...] be [...] words are pri[...]
in bold he[...] type [...] [...]word[...]
printed in [...]

How to sa[...]
We have [...]
nounced. [...]
quite unli[...]ny so[...] [...]on [...]book[...]
it better t[...] [...]ou [...] [...]ny gr[...]
up who sp[...] [...]e [...] [...]s word[...]
this book [...] [...] [...] [...] a Fr[...]
person!

B297

THIS BOOK BELONGS TO

Lizzy Sega[...]

Masculines and Feminines
In English we say "a boy" and "a girl" or "the boy" and "the girl." In French they say **un garçon** and **une fille** or **le garçon** and **la fille**. **Garçon** is, as you might expect, a masculine word and **un** in French is the masculine for "a." The masculine for "the" is **le** in French. In the same way **une** in French is the feminine for "a," and **la** is the feminine for "the."

In French **all** words are either masculine or feminine. For example "the sun" is masculine (**le soleil** in French) but "the snow" is feminine (**la neige** in French). If the word is plural then in French **le** and **la** both become **les**, (**les livres** for the books, and **les chaises** for the chairs).

Concept: John Grisewood
French translators: Peter Barber
Jean-Pierre Hénot (École Primaire de Beaurainville)
Spanish translators: Raquel-Moya-Agudo
Kevin Hughes (Language Dept.
High Peak College of Further Education)

CONTENTS

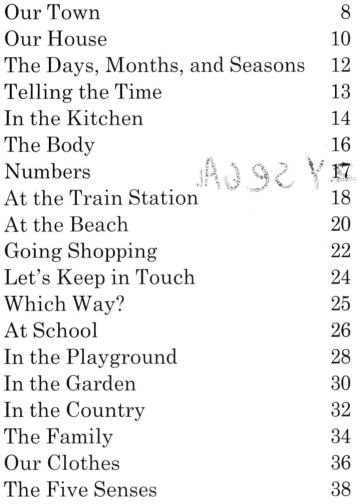

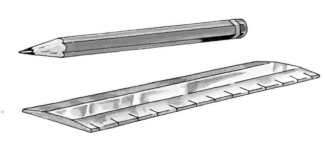

Our Town

1. **road** — la chaussée
2. **sidewalk** — le trottoir
3. **subway station** — une station de métro
4. **telephone booth** — une cabine téléphonique
5. **hotel** — un hôtel
6. **post office** — le bureau de poste
7. **trash can** — une boite à ordures
8. **drugstore** — la pharmacie
9. **policeman** — un agent de police
10. **baker** — une boulangerie
11. **supermarket** — un supermarché
12. **offices** — les bureaux
13. **movie theater** — le cinéma
14. **apartments** — les appartements
15. **bank** — une banque
16. **lamppost** — un revérbère
17. **traffic lights** — les feux
18. **car** — une voiture
19. **parking meter** — un parcomètre
20. **truck** — un camion

Our House

1.	**antenna**	une antenne
2.	**roof**	le toit
3.	**chimney**	la cheminée
4.	**attic**	le grenier
5.	**bathroom**	la salle de bains
6.	**toothbrush**	une brosse à dents
7.	**towel**	une serviette
8.	**soap**	le savon
9.	**bed**	un lit
10.	**pillow**	un oreiller
11.	**window**	une fenêtre
12.	**ceiling**	le plafond
13.	**floor**	le plancher
14.	**stairs**	l'escalier
15.	**lamp**	une lampe
16.	**living room**	le salon
17.	**sofa**	un canapé
18.	**picture**	un tableau
19.	**chair**	une chaise
20.	**kitchen**	la cuisine
21.	**tent**	une tente
22.	**bone**	un os

11

The Days, Months, and Seasons

What is your favorite time of year?

THE SEASONS   LES SAISONS

Spring
Le printemps

It's a nice day.
Il fait beau.

Summer
L'été

It is warm.
Il fait chaud.

Autumn
L'automne

It is windy.
Il fait du vent.

Winter
L'hiver

Il fait froid.

1.	**rain**	la pluie
2.	**blossom**	les fleurs des arbres
3.	**rainbow**	un arc-en-ciel
4.	**sun**	le soleil
5.	**cloud**	un nuage
6.	**wind**	le vent
7.	**leaves falling**	les feuilles qui tombent
8.	**snow**	la neige
9.	**snowman**	un bonhomme de neige

THE MONTHS	LES MOIS	DAYS OF THE WEEK	LES JOURS DE LA SEMAINE
January	janvier	**Monday**	lundi
February	février	**Tuesday**	mardi
March	mars	**Wednesday**	mercredi
April	avril	**Thursday**	jeudi
May	mai	**Friday**	vendredi
June	juin	**Saturday**	samedi
July	juillet	**Sunday**	dimanche
August	août		
September	septembre		
October	octobre		
November	novembre		
December	décembre		

Telling the Time

What's the time?
Quelle heure est-il?

It's seven o'clock. Time to get up.
Il est sept heures. C'est l'heure de me lever.

It's eight-thirty. Time for school.
Il est huit heures et demie. L'heure de l'école.

alarm clock
un réveil

yesterday
hier

morning
le matin

It is twelve noon. Lunch time.
Il est midi. L'heure du déjeuner.

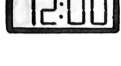

afternoon
l'après-midi

wrist watch
une montre

It's a quarter to eight. Story time.
Il est huit heures moins le quart. L'heure de raconter une histoire.

today
aujourd'hui

evening
le soir

It's a quarter past eight. Bedtime.
Il est huit heures et quart. L'heure d'aller au lit.

clock
une pendule

It is midnight. It is dark outside.
Il est minuit. Dehors, il fait noir.

night
la nuit

tomorrow
demain

13

In the Kitchen

1.	**sink**	l'évier
2.	**faucet**	un robinet
3.	**can-opener**	un ouvre-boîtes
4.	**vegetable rack**	un casier à légumes
5.	**electric mixer**	un batteur éléctrique
6.	**washing machine**	une machine à laver
7.	**dishwasher**	un lave-vaisselle
8.	**rolling pin**	un rouleau
9.	**garbage can**	une poubelle
10.	**refrigerator**	un réfrigérateur
11.	**broom**	un balai
12.	**saucepan**	une casserole
13.	**frying pan**	une poêle
14.	**stove**	une cuisinière
15.	**table**	une table
16.	**stool**	un tabouret
17.	**coffee pot**	une cafetière
18.	**bowl**	un bol
19.	**pitcher**	un pot
20.	**iron**	un fer
21.	**ironing board**	une planche à repasser
22.	**cup and saucer**	une tasse et une soucoupe

The Body
From Head to Toe.

foot
le pied

back
le dos

face
la figure

shoulder
l'épaule

leg
la jambe

stomach
l'estomac

chest
la poitrine

arm
le bras

hand
la main

head
la tête

Come on in! The water is lovely!
Viens! L'eau est bonne!

1. **mouth**   la bouche
2. **nose**   le nez
3. **eye (eyes)**   l'oeil (les yeux)
4. **ear**   l'oreille
5. **hair**   les cheveux
6. **neck**   le cou
7. **elbow**   le coude
8. **finger**   le doigt
9. **thumb**   le pouce
10. **knee**   le genou
11. **ankle**   la cheville
12. **toe**   l'orteil

Numbers
Can you count up to 20?

How many can you count?
Il y en a combien?

There is one elephant and there are...
Il y a un éléphant et il y a...

1. **one elephant** — un éléphant
2. **two sandals** — deux sandales
3. **three teddy bears** — trois nounours
4. **four penguins** — quatre pingouins
5. **five mice** — cinq souris
6. **six ice creams** — six glaces
7. **seven balloons** — sept ballons
8. **eight fish** — huit poissons
9. **nine strawberries** — neuf fraises
10. **ten keys** — dix clés
11. **eleven mushrooms** — onze champignons
12. **twelve eggs** — douze oeufs
13. **thirteen ladybugs** — treize coccinelles
14. **fourteen cupcakes** — quatorze gâteaux
15. **fifteen thumbtacks** — quinze punaises
16. **sixteen flowers** — seize fleurs
17. **seventeen matches** — dix-sept alumettes
18. **eighteen bricks** — dix-huits briques
19. **nineteen buttons** — dix-neufs boutons
20. **twenty ants** — vingt fourmis

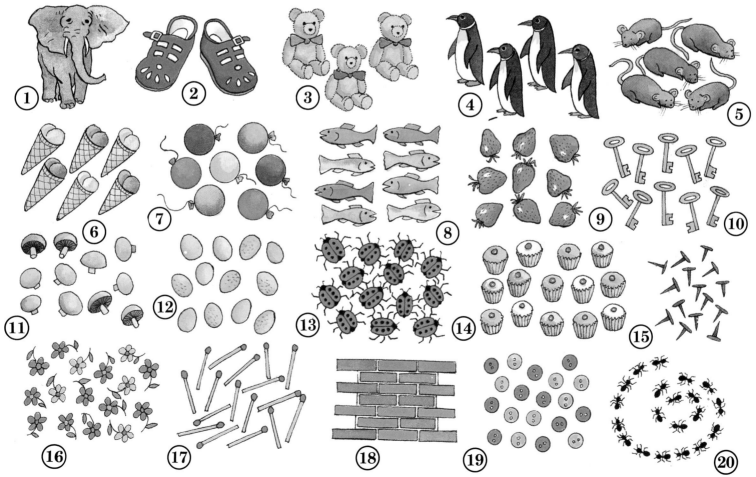

At the Train Station

1.	**train**	un train
2.	**engineer**	le conducteur
3.	**locomotive**	une locomotive
4.	**railroad track**	la voie ferée
5.	**platform**	le quai
6.	**car**	un wagon
7.	**guard**	le chef de train
8.	**flag**	un drapeau
9.	**porter**	un porteur
10.	**luggage trolley**	un chariot à bagages
11.	**luggage**	les bagages
12.	**passenger**	un voyageur
13.	**signal**	un signal
14.	**exit**	la sortie
15.	**subway**	un souterrain
16.	**newspaper**	un journal
17.	**news vendor**	un marchand de journaux
18.	**handbag**	un sac à main
19.	**platform number**	le numéro du quai
20.	**refreshment stand**	un buffet

At the Beach

1.	**sky**	le ciel
2.	**sun**	le soleil
3.	**cloud**	un nuage
4.	**sand**	le sable
5.	**sea**	la mer
6.	**wave**	une vague
7.	**cliff**	une falaise
8.	**cave**	une caverne
9.	**seagull**	une mouette
10.	**yacht**	un voilier
11.	**sail**	une voile
12.	**mast**	un mât
13.	**rowboat**	un bateau à rames
14.	**motor boat**	une vedette
15.	**fish**	un poisson
16.	**surfer**	un surfeur
17.	**rock**	un rocher
18.	**seaweed**	le varech
19.	**ship**	un navire
20.	**pail**	un seau
21.	**shovel**	une pelle
22.	**raft**	un radeau
23.	**umbrella**	un parasol
24.	**deck chair**	un transatlantique
25.	**lighthouse**	un phare

We are building a sandcastle.
Nous faisons un château en sable.

No. But I can swim.
Non, mais je sais nager.

Can you dive?
Tu sais plonger?

crab
un crabe

ice cream
une glace

shell
une coquille

Going Shopping

1. **fruit** — les fruits
2. **vegetables** — les légumes
3. **meat** — la viande
4. **fish** — le poisson
5. **bread** — le pain
6. **cake** — le gâteau
7. **sugar** — le sucre
8. **milk** — le lait
9. **eggs** — les oeufs
10. **cheese** — le fromage
11. **butter** — le beurre
12. **pears** — les poires
13. **apples** — les pommes
14. **bananas** — les bananes
15. **potatoes** — les pommes de terres
16. **onions** — les oignons
17. **carrots** — les carottes
18. **cauliflower** — un chou-fleur
19. **wine** — le vin
20. **checkout** — la caisse
21. **shopping cart** — un chariot
22. **cashier** — la caissière
23. **money** — l'argent

strawberry une fraise

raspberry une framboise

lemon un citron

mushroom un champignon

Thank you. How much is it?
Merci. C'est combien?

I would like to buy a package of candy, please.
Je voudrais un paquet de bonbons, s'il vous plaît.

Let's keep in touch

1. **newspaper**   un journal
2. **books**   les livres
3. **television**   un téléviseur
4. **radio**   la radio
5. **typewriter**   une machine à écrire
6. **letter**   une lettre
7. **envelope**   une enveloppe
8. **stamp**   un timbre-poste
9. **address**   une adresse
10. **pen**   un stylo
11. **photograph**   une photographie
12. **telephone**   un téléphone
13. **camera**   un appareil
14. **calculator**   une calculatrice

Which Way?

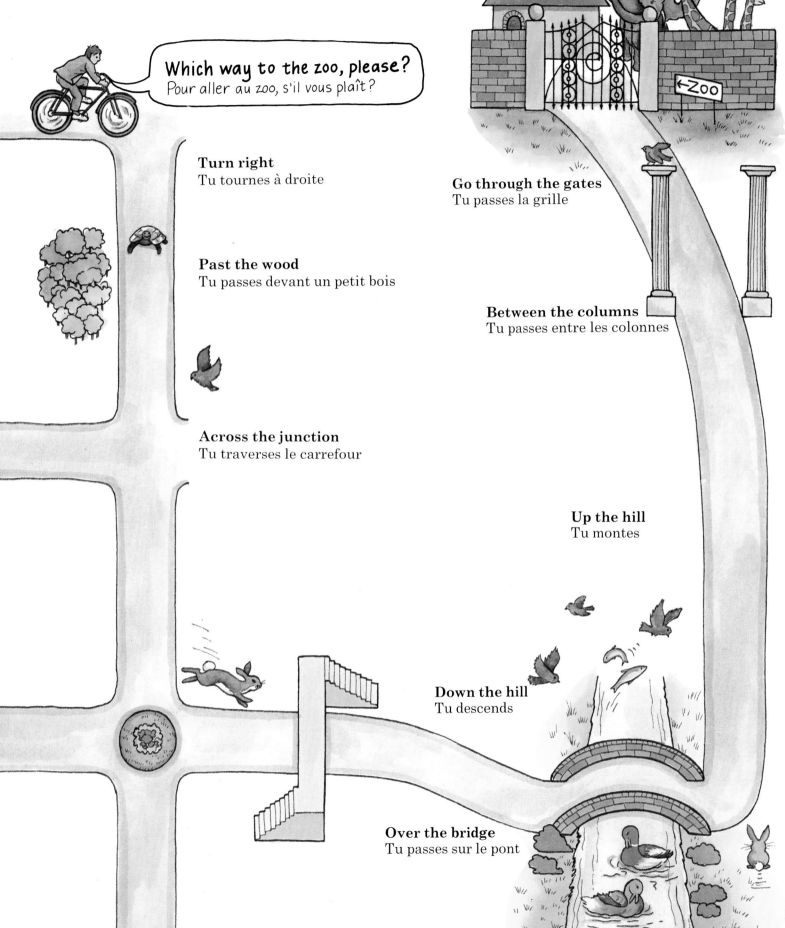

Which way to the zoo, please?
Pour aller au zoo, s'il vous plaît ?

Turn right
Tu tournes à droite

Past the wood
Tu passes devant un petit bois

Across the junction
Tu traverses le carrefour

Go through the gates
Tu passes la grille

Between the columns
Tu passes entre les colonnes

Up the hill
Tu montes

Down the hill
Tu descends

Over the bridge
Tu passes sur le pont

25

At School

1. **blackboard** — un tableau noir
2. **globe** — un globe terrestre
3. **easel** — un chevalet
4. **abacus** — un abaque
5. **teacher** — une institutrice
6. **pupil (boy)** — un écolier
   pupil (girl) — une écolière
7. **paints** — les couleurs
8. **paintbrushes** — les pinceaux
9. **painting** — la peinture
10. **exercise book** — un cahier
11. **paper** — le papier
12. **alphabet** — l'alphabet
13. **sums** — le calcul
14. **school bag** — un cartable
15. **wastepaper basket** — une corbeille à papier
16. **cupboard** — une armoire
17. **chalk** — la craie
18. **goldfish** — un poisson rouge
19. **books** — les livres

It's easy to learn how to speak English.

Apprendre l'anglais, ce n'est pas difficile.

pencil sharpener
un taille-crayons

thumb tack
une punaise

scissors
les ciseaux

ruler
une régle

pencil
un crayon

Can you teach me to paint?
Je voudrais savoir peindre.

In the Playground

1. **walk**   marcher
2. **stand**   se tenir debout
3. **jump**   sauter
4. **skip**   sauter à la corde
5. **sit**   être assis
6. **run**   courir
7. **throw**   lancer
8. **catch**   attraper
9. **pull**   tirer
10. **push**   pousser
11. **fall down**   tomber
12. **eat**   manger
13. **drink**   boire
14. **wave**   faire signe
15. **smile**   sourire
16. **cry**   pleurer
17. **read**   lire
18. **bend**   se pencher
19. **hop**   sauter à cloche-pied
20. **climb**   grimper
21. **give**   donner
22. **take**   prendre
23. **speak**   parler
24. **listen**   écouter

play
jouer

Do you speak English?
Parlez-vous anglais?

No, but
Non, mais . . .

I speak French	Je parle français
You speak German	Tu parles allemand
He speaks Spanish	Il parle espagnol.
She speaks Chinese	Elle parle chinois
We speak Italian	Nous parlons italien
You speak Russian	Vous parlez russe
They speak Portuguese	Ils parlent portugais
They speak Swedish	Elles parlent suédois

In the Garden

1. **tree** — un arbre
2. **leaf** — une feuille
3. **bush** — un arbuste
4. **grass** — le gazon
5. **lawnmower** — une tondeuse
6. **flowerbed** — une plate-bande
7. **worm** — un ver
8. **wheelbarrow** — une brouette
9. **watering can** — un arrosoir
10. **greenhouse** — une serre
11. **spade** — une bêche
12. **pitchfork** — une fourche
13. **swing** — une balançoire
14. **seesaw** — une bascule
15. **fence** — une clôture
16. **vegetables** — les légumes
17. **hose** — un tuyau
18. **earth** — la terre
19. **pond** — un bassin
20. **path** — une allée

rose
une rose

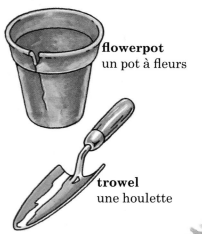

flowerpot
un pot à fleurs

trowel
une houlette

In the Country

1. **farmhouse** — une maison de ferme
2. **farmer** — le fermier
3. **chickens** — les poulets
4. **pig** — un cochon
5. **cow** — une vache
6. **calf** — un veau
7. **sheep** — un mouton
8. **lamb** — un agneau
9. **hill** — une colline
10. **mountain** — une montagne
11. **village** — un village
12. **wood** — un bois
13. **horse** — un cheval
14. **tractor** — un tracteur
15. **plow** — une charrue
16. **turkey** — un dindon
17. **fox** — un renard
18. **hedge** — une haie
19. **rabbit** — un lapin
20. **squirrel** — un écureuil

milk le lait
cheese le fromage
butter la beurre

The Family

The whole family is arriving to wish Grandma a happy birthday.

cat
un chat

kitten
un chaton

dog
un chien

puppy
un chiot

duck
un canard

duckling
un caneton

1. **mother (mommy)** — la mère (maman)
2. **father (daddy)** — le père (papa)
3. **baby** — le bébé
4. **daughter** — la fille
5. **son** — le fils
6. **grandmother/wife** — la grand-mère/la femme
7. **grandfather/husband** — le grand-père/le mari
8. **grandchildren** — les petits-enfants
9. **uncle** — l'oncle
10. **aunt** — la tante
11. **cousin** — le cousin (boy) la cousine (girl)
12. **brother** — le frère
13. **sister** — la soeur
14. **nephew** — le neveu
15. **niece** — la nièce
16. **present** — un cadeau
17. **flowers** — les fleurs

This is my brother. I am his sister. We belong to the same family.
Voici mon frère. Je suis sa soeur. Nous sommes de la même famille.

Our Clothes

1.	**dress**	une robe
2.	**skirt**	une jupe
3.	**jeans**	un jean
4.	**socks**	les chaussettes
5.	**shoes**	les chaussures
6.	**gloves**	les gants
7.	**hat**	un chapeau
8.	**sweater**	un chandail
9.	**belt**	une ceinture
10.	**jacket**	un veston
11.	**pants**	un pantalon
12.	**underpants**	un slip
13.	**undershirt**	un maillot de corps
14.	**shirt**	une chemise
15.	**tie**	une cravate
16.	**pajamas**	un pyjama
17.	**bathrobe**	un peignoir
18.	**slippers**	les pantoufles
19.	**raincoat**	un imperméable
20.	**overcoat**	un pardessus
21.	**clothes closet**	une garde-robe
22.	**mirror**	une glace/un miroir
23.	**hanger**	un cintre

handkerchief
un mouchoir

comb
un peigne

hairbrush
une brosse à cheveux

The Five Senses

sight
la vue

Look at the balloon in the sky. Can you see it?
Regarde le ballon dans le ciel. Tu peux le voir?

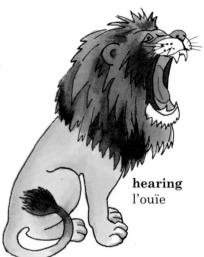

Listen to the lion roaring. Can you hear him?
Écoute le lion qui rugit. Tu peux l'entendre?

hearing
l'ouïe

smell
l'odorat

Smell the flowers. Can you smell the scent?
Sens les fleurs. Tu peux en sentir l'odeur?

Taste the ice-cream. Can you taste the chocolate?
Goûte la glace. Tu peux en sentir le parfum de chocolat?

taste
le goût

Touch the cat's fur. Can you feel how soft it is?
Touche la fourrure du chat. Tu peux sentir comme elle est douce?

touch
le toucher

Touch the table. Can you feel how hard it is?
Touche la table. Tu peux sentir comme elle est dure?

Shapes and Colors
When you mix colors together you make new colors.

a pink rectangle
un rectangle rose

a red circle
un cercle rouge

a black oval
un ovale noir

a white square
un carré blanc

a yellow star
une étoile jaune

a blue sphere
une sphère bleue

a purple heart
un coeur violet

a brown cube
un cube brun

an orange pyramid
une pyramide orange

Blue and yellow make green.
Le bleu et le jaune produisent le vert

WORD LIST

bird
un oiseau

ENGLISH	FRENCH
abacus	un abaque
address	une adresse
afternoon	un après-midi
airplane	un avion
airport	un aéroport
alarm clock	un réveil
alphabet	un alphabet
ankle	la cheville
ant	un fourmi
antenna	une antenne
apple	une pomme
April	avril
arm	le bras
attic	un grenier
August	août
aunt	une tante
autumn	automne
baby	un bébé
bakery	une boulangerie
balloon	un ballon
banana	une banane
bank	une banque
to bark	aboyer
bathroom	une salle de bains
bed	un lit
bell (small, hand-)	une sonnette
belt	une ceinture
to bend	st pencher
between	entre
bicycle	un vélo
bird	un oiseau
black	noir, noire
blackboard	un tableau noir
blossom	les fleures des arbres
blue	bleu, bleue
body	le corps
bone	un os
book	un livre
bowl	un bol
boy	un garçon
brake	un frein
bread	le pain
breakfast	le petit déjeuner
brick	une brique
bridge	un pont
broom	un balai
brother	un frère
brown	brun, brune
bucket	un seau
to build	construire, faire
bush	un arbuste
but	mais
butter	le beurre
button	un bouton
to buy	acheter
cake	un gâteau
calculator	une calculatrice
calendar	un calendrier
calf	un veau
camera	un appareil (photographique)

can (= to be able to, know how to)	savoir
can opener	un ouvre-boîtes
car	une automobile, une voiture
car (railroad)	le wagon
carrot	une carotte
cashier	une caissière
cat	un chat
to catch	attraper
cauliflower	un chou-fleur
cave	une caverne
ceiling	un plafond
chair	une chaise
chalk	la craie
checkout (supermarket)	une caisse
cheese	un fromage
chest (part of body)	la poitrine
chicken	un poulet
child	un enfant
chimney	une cheminée
circle	un cercle
classroom	une salle de classe
cliff	une falaise
to climb	grimper
clock (household)	une pendule
cloth	une étoffe
clothes	les vêtements
cloud	un nuage
coffee pot	une cafetière
cold	froid, froide

balloon
un ballon

airplane
un avion

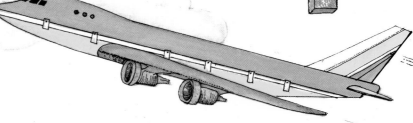

control tower
une tour de contrôle

color	une couleur
comb	un peigne
control tower (airport)	une tour de contrôle
cooker	une cuisinière
corkscrew	un tire-bouchon
corner	un coin
to count	compter
cousin	un cousin, une cousine
cow	une vache
crab	un crabe
to cry	pleurer
cube	un cube
cup	une tasse
cupboard	une armoire
dad, daddy	papa
(it is) dark	il fait noir
date	la date
daughter	une fille
day	un jour
December	décembre
deck chair	un transatlantique
to dig	bêcher
dishwasher	un lave-vaisselle
to dive	plonger
to do	faire
dog	un chien
door	une porte
to draw	dessiner
drawer	un tiroir
dress	une robe
to drink	boire
duck	un canard
ear	une oreille
earth	la terre
easel	un chevalet
to eat	manger
egg	un oeuf
eight	huit
eighteen	dix-huit
elbow	le coude
electric mixer	un batteur électrique
elephant	un éléphant
eleven	onze
envelope	une enveloppe
eraser	une gomme
evening	un soir
exercise book	un cahier
exit	la sortie
eye, eyes	l'oeil, les yeux
face	la figure, le visage
to fall	tomber
family	une famille
farm/farmhouse	une ferme/une maison ferme
farmer	un fermier
father	le père
February	février
fence	une clôture
fifteen	quinze
finger	le doigt
fish	un poisson

glider
un planeur

five	cinq
flag	un drapeau
floor	un plancher
flower	une fleur
flowerbed	une plate-bande
flowerpot	un pot à fleurs
foot	le pied
fork (table)	une fourchette
four	quatre
fourteen	quatorze
fox	un renard
Friday	vendredi
friend	un ami, une amie
fruit	un fruit
frying-pan	une poêle (à frire)
garden	un jardin
gate	une barrière; une grille
to give	donner
glider	un planeur
globe (in classroom)	un globe terrestre
glove	un gant
to go	aller
goldfish	un poisson rouge
grandchildren	les petits-enfants
grandfather	un grand-père
grandmother/*granny	une grand-mère/grand-maman
grass	le gazon/l'herbe
green	vert, verte
greenhouse	une serre
guard (train)	un chef de train
hair	les cheveux
half	la moitié
hand	la main
handbag	un sac à main
handkerchief	un mouchoir
handlebar	un guidon
hanger	un cintre
hat	un chapeau
to have	avoir
head	la tête
to hear	entendre
heart	le coeur
hedge	une haie
helicopter	un hélicoptère
hill	une colline

helicopter
un hélicoptère

to hop	sauter à cloche-pied
horse	un cheval
hose (garden)	un tuyau
hot	chaud, chaude
hotel	un hôtel
hour	une heure
house	une maison
hungry/I'm hungry	faim/j'ai faim
husband	un mari
I/I'm a boy	je/je suis un garçon
ice	la glace
ice cream	une glace
iron	un fer à repasser
ironing board	une planche à repasser
it's	c'est
jacket	un veston
January	janvier
jeans	un jean, un blue-jean
jet engine	un moteur à réaction
jug	un pot
July	juillet
to jump	sauter
June	juin
kennel	une niche
kettle	une bouilloire
key	une clé, une clef
kitchen	une cuisine
kite	un cerf-volant
kitten	un chaton
knee	le genou
knife	un couteau
ladybug	un coccinelle
lamb	un agneau
lamp	une lampe
lamppost	un réverbère
lawnmower	une tondeuse
leaf	une feuille
to learn	apprendre
to leave	partir, quitter
left	la gauche
leg	la jambe
lemon	un citron
letter	une lettre
lighthouse	un phare
lion	le lion
to listen	écouter
living-room	une salle de séjour
to look	regarder
luggage	les bagages
to make	faire
man	un homme
March	mars
mast	un mât
match	une alumette
May	mai
meat	la viande

kite
un cerf-volant

midnight	minuit
milk	le lait
mirror	un miroir, une glace
mommy	maman
Monday	lundi
money	l'argent
month	un mois
moon	la lune
morning	le matin
mother	la mère
motor boat	une vedette
mountain	une montagne
mouse	un souris
mouth	la bouche
movie theater	un cinéma
mushroom	un champignon
my	mon, ma, mes (mon oncle/ma tante/mes jouets)
name	un nom
neck	le cou
nest	un nid
nephew	le neveu
newspaper	un journal
niece	la nièce
night	une nuit
nine	neuf
nineteen	dix-neuf
noon	midi
nose	le nez
November	novembre
number	un chiffre, un numéro
October	octobre
office	un bureau
one	un, une
onion	un oignon
orange (color)	orange
oval	un ovale, ovale
overcoat	un pardessus

package	un paquet	rock	un rocher
to paint	peindre	rolling pin	un rouleau
paintbrush	un pinceau	roof	un toit
painting	une peinture	rose	une rose
pajamas	un pyjama	rowboat	un bateau à rames
paper	le papier	ruler	une règle
parking meter	un parcomètre	to run	courir
passenger	un voyageur, une voyageuse	runway	une piste d'envol
path (garden)	une allée	saddle	une selle
pear	une poire	sail	une voile
pedal	une pédale	sand	le sable
pen	un stylo	sandal	la sandale
pencil	un crayon	Saturday	samedi
pencil sharpener	un taille-crayon	saucer	une soucoupe
penguin	un pingouin	saucepan	une casserole
people	les gens	scales (pair of)	une balance
pet	un animal familier	school	une école
pharmacy	une pharmacie	scissors	les ciseaux
photograph	une photographie	sea	la mer
piano	un piano	seagull	une mouette
picture	un tableau	seaweed	le varech
pig	un cochon	seesaw	une bascule
pillow	un oreiller	September	septembre
pink	rose	seven	sept
pitchfork	une fourche	seventeen	dix-sept
plant	une plante	she	elle
plate	une assiette	sheep	un mouton
platform	un quai	shelf	un rayon
to play	jouer	shell	une coquille
please	s'il te plaît, s'il vous plaît	ship	un navire
plow	une charrue	shirt	une chemise
policeman	un agent (de police)	shoes	les chaussures, les souliers
pond (garden)	un bassin	to shut	fermer
porter	un porteur	sidewalk	un trottoir
post office	un bureau de poste	to sing	chanter
potato	une pomme de terre	singer	un chanteur, une chanteuse
present	un cadeau		
to pull	tirer	sink (kitchen)	un évier
pupil (primary school)	un écolier, une écolière	sister	une soeur
pupil (secondary school)	un élève, une élève	to sit (be seated)	être assis (be seated); s'asseoir (to sit down)
puppy	un chiot		
purple	violet, violette	six	six
to push	pousser	sixteen	seize
pyramid	une pyramide	skip (with jump rope)	sauter à la corde
		skirt	une jupe
rabbit	un lapin	sky	le ciel
radio	une radio	to sleep	dormir; s'endormir (to go to sleep)
raft	un radeau		
railroad track	la voie ferrée	slipper	une pantoufle
rain	la pluie	to smell (a flower etc)	sentir
rainbow	un arc-en-ciel	to smile	sourire
raincoat	un imperméable	snow	la neige
raspberry	une framboise	snowman	un bonhomme de neige
to read	lire	soap	le savon
rectangle	un rectangle	sock	la chaussette
red	rouge	sofa	un canapé
refreshment stand	un buffet	soft	doux, douce
refrigerator	un réfrigérateur, un frigo	son	un fils
to ride (= to go horse riding)	faire de l'équitation	spade	une bêche (garden); une pelle (seaside)
right	la droite	to speak	parler
river	une rivière, un fleuve		
road	la chaussée/une route		

spoon	une cuillère	towel	une serviette
spring (season)	le printemps	town	une ville
square	un carré	tractor	un tracteur
squirrel	un écureuil	traffic lights	les feux (de circulation)
stairs	un escalier	train	un train
stamp (postage)	un timbre-poste	trash can	une boite à ordures
to stand (= to be	être debout, se tenir	tree	un arbre
standing)	debout (to be standing);	triangle	un triangle
	se lever (to get up)	trolley (supermarket)	un chariot
station	la gare	trowel	une houlette
star	une étoile	Tuesday	mardi
stomach	l'estomac	turkey	un dindon, une dinde
stool	un tabouret	to turn	tourner
to stop	s'arrêter	twelve	douze
stawberry	une fraise	twenty	vingt
street	une rue	two	deux
sugar	le sucre	typewriter	une machine à écrire
summer	l'été		
sun	le soleil	umbrella (beach)	un parasol
Sunday	dimanche	uncle	un oncle
supermarket	un supermarché	underpants	un slip
sweater	un chandail	vegetables	les légumes
to swim	nager	very	très
swing	une balançoire	village	un village
table	une table	to wake (up)	se réveiller
tail	une queue	to walk	marcher
to take	prendre	to want	vouloir
to talk	parler	washing machine	une machine à laver
tap	un robinet	wastepaper basket	une corbeille à papier
to taste	goûter	water	l'eau
taste (sense of)	le goût	watering can	un arrosoir
taxi	un taxi	wave (sea)	une vague
to teach	enseigner	wave	faire signe
teacher (primary school)	un instituteur,	we	nous
	une institutrice	to wear	porter
Teddy (-bear)	un nounours	Wednesday	mercredi
telephone	un téléphone	week	une semaine
telephone booth	une cabine téléphonique	what . . ?/what are you	qu'est-ce que . .?/qu'est-
television set	un téléviseur	eating?	ce que tu manges?
ten	dix	wheel	une roue
tennis	le tennis	wheelbarrow	une brouette
tent	une tente	where?	où?
there is, there are	il y a	white	blanc, blanche
they	ils, elles	wife	une femme
thirteen	treize	wind	le vent
three	trois	window	une fenêtre
to throw	lancer, jeter	wine	un vin
thumb	le pouce	wing	une aile
Thursday	jeudi	winter	l'hiver
ticket	un ticket (bus, subway); el billete	woman	une femme
	un billet (railway,	wood	un bois
	theater)	wool	la laine
tie	une cravate	worm	un ver
time	l'heure	wristwatch	une montre
tire	un pneu	to write	écrire
tired	fatigué, fatiguée		
today	aujourd'hui	yacht	un voilier
toe	le doigt de pied, l'orteil	year	un an, une année
tomorrow	demain	yellow	jaune
tooth	la dent	yesterday	ñier
toothbrush	une brosse à dents		
touch (sense of)	le toucher	zoo	un jardin zoologique, un zoo

I am writing a letter to Maria.
J'écris à Maria.

"Thank you for your letter."
"Je te remercie de ta lettre."

"How are you? I am very well."
"Comment vas-tu? Moi, je vais bien."

"Goodnight for now."
"Bonne nuit"

"I have a new pet. It is a hamster called Otto."
"J'ai un nouveau petit animal. C'est un hamster qui s'appelle Otto."

"It is very quiet tonight."
"Ce soir, tout est tranquille."

"I am tired and sleepy."
"Moi, je suis fatigué, j'ai sommeil."